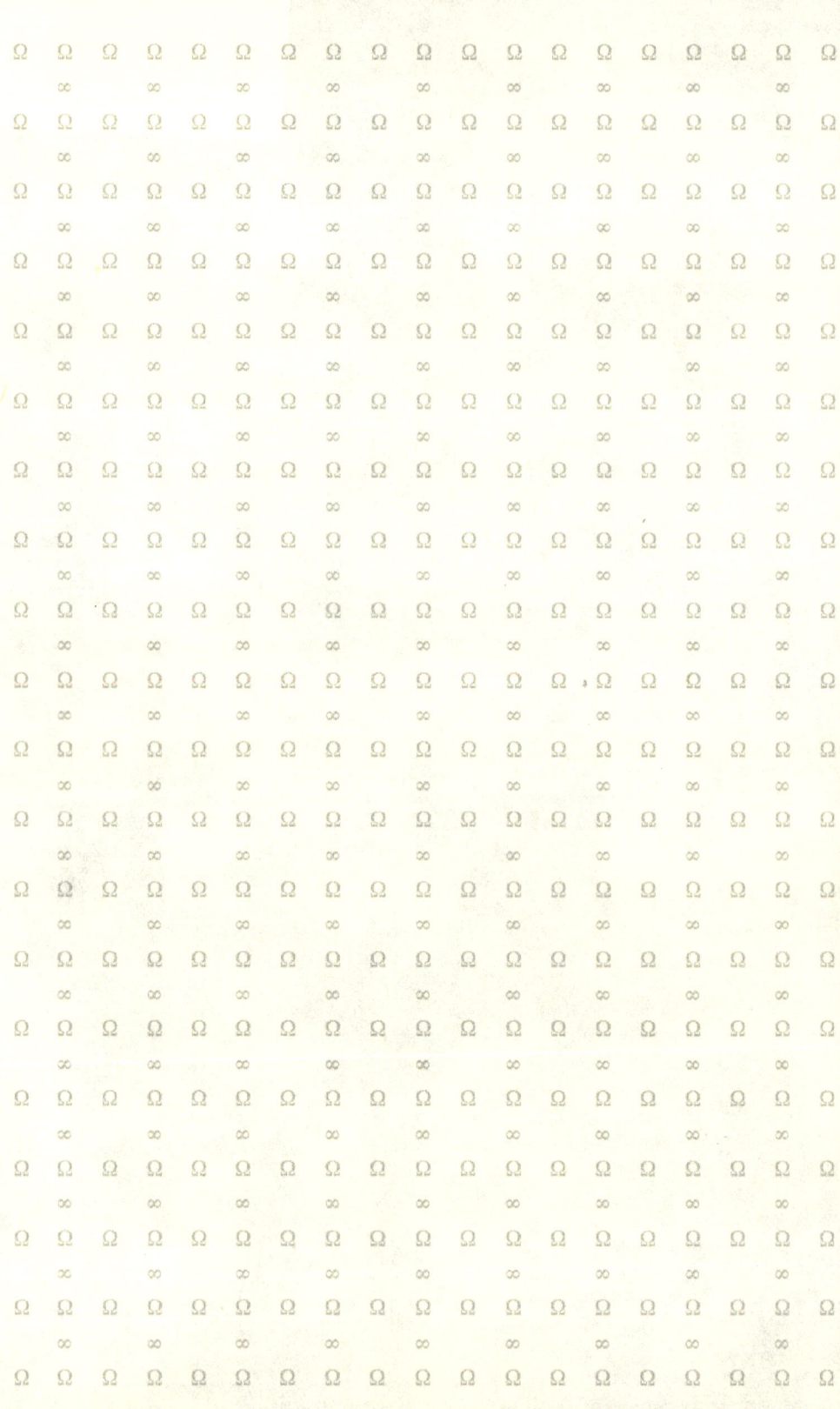

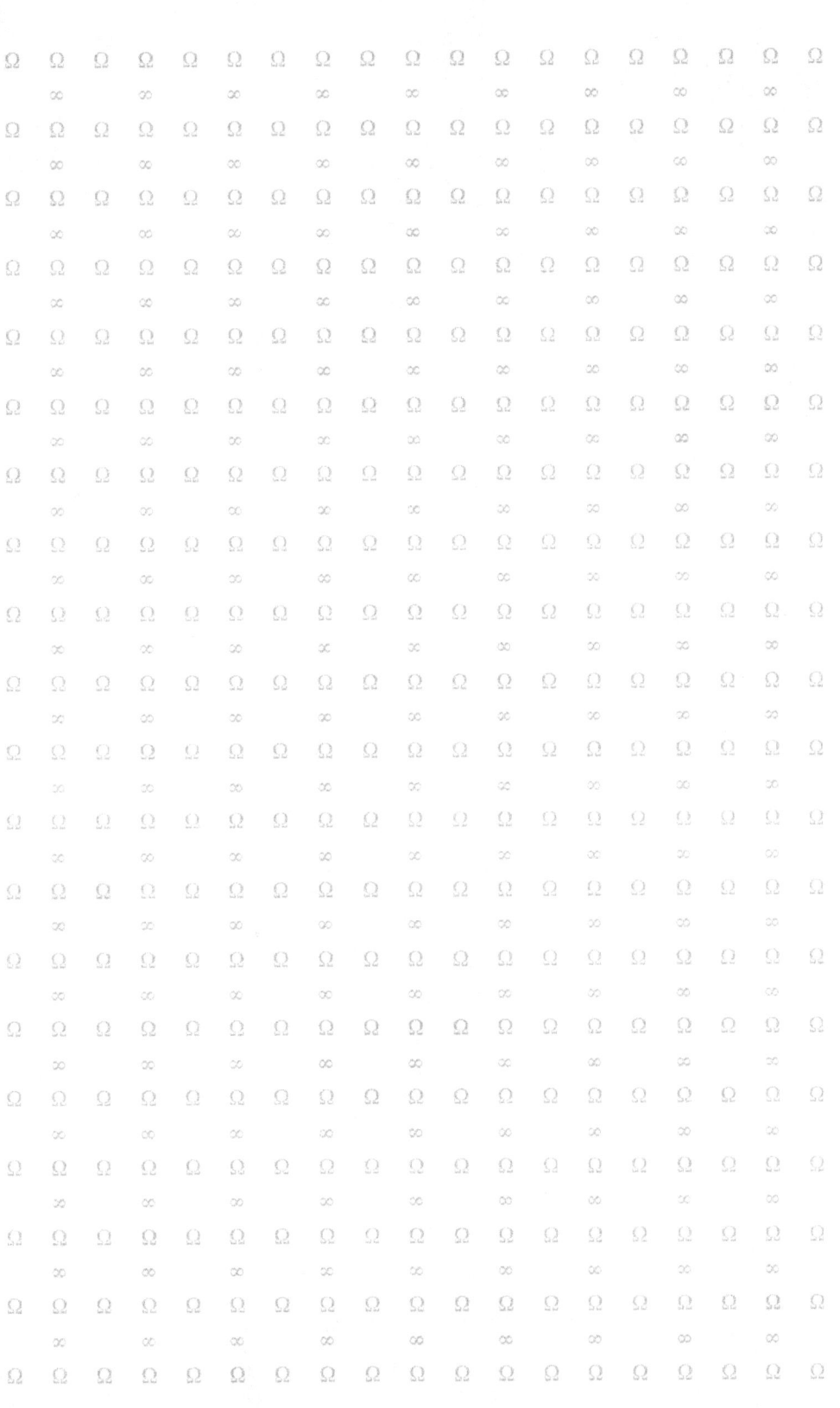

Love Bird

Georgie Harriss

Published by in case of emergency press 2022

Copyright © Georgie Harriss 2022

All rights reserved. Without limiting the rights under copyright reserved above, no part of this publication may be reproduced, stored in or introduced into a database and retrieval system or transmitted in any form or any means (electronic, mechanical, photocopying, recording or otherwise) without the prior written permission of both the owner of copyright and the above publishers.

Cover and Title Page photo **Ursula Gamez** *Unsplash.com*

ISBN 978-0-6451280-5-5

in case of emergency press

We are proud to acknowledge the Traditional Owners of country throughout Australia and to recognise their continuing connection to land, waters, and culture.

We pay our respects to their Elders.

We support recognition, reconciliation, and reparation.

Reviews of *Love Bird*

'Harriss is on par with the Wes Andersons of the world' (Stage Whispers)

'Harriss... has a serious penchant for delving into the dark side of the family unit and teasing out its tensions and anxieties, and actually making people laugh' (Stage Whispers)

'Harriss has a talent for searching the depths of the family soul then baring it to the world with flagrant absurdity that had one's giggle buttons hit continuously' (TAGG)

'Georgina has written an extremely funny script with humorous, often subtle, lines woven into each character's dialogue' (Melbourne Observer)

'Plenty of laughs with moments that will surprise and strangely delight audiences' (My Melbourne Arts)

'Harriss is not afraid to dive deep into realms of the taboo, immersing audience members in truly uncomfortable subject matter that is thankfully offset by liberal amounts of slapstick and humour' (Milkbar Mag)

'Love Bird may push the envelope with what it depicts on stage, but look beyond the bestiality and Harriss has something meaningful and insightful to impart' (My Melbourne Arts)

'...a very dangerous work' (Samsara Dunston)

Table of Contents

Introduction by the Author	i
Production History	iv
Act 1	**1**
Scene 1	1
Scene 2	6
Scene 3	9
Scene 4	10
Scene 5	13
Scene 6	15
Scene 7	18
Scene 8	20
ACT 2	**24**
Scene 1	24
Scene 2	27
Scene 3	28
Scene 4	30
ACT 3	**33**
Scene 1	33
Scene 2	36
Scene 3	39
Scene 4	41
Scene 5	42
Scene 6	43
About the Author	**45**

Love Bird

Georgie Harriss

in case of emergency press
https://icoe.com.au
Travancore
Australia

Introduction by the Author

I'm sorry to say the play you're about to read is semi-autobiographical. As a small mercy or a minor cruelty—which one, only you the reader can decide—I will not disclose which aspects of the tale are fictional and which are not. What I will tell you is that this play is based upon the very real relationship I had with my childhood cockatiel, Ping Pong, who was named after the only sport in which I almost excelled.

It's a tale as old as time: bird meets girl, they have a great time together, they share moments of profound emotional intimacy, things get physical and then... things get complicated. Little did my parents know, solitary cockatiels are notorious for forming inappropriate sexual attachments to their owners, a tendency that causes countless frustrations for both the bird and their human family.

In retrospect, Ping Pong could be said to have set a lot of precedents that I encountered in my future romantic endeavours. He was wildly jealous, he asserted his needs ahead of my own and he instilled in me that sense of sweet relief that comes from satisfying another's sexual cravings just so they'll get off your back about it.

But the truth is, blaming Ping Pong for any of these lessons learnt is entirely unfair and therein lies the injustice of our everyday anthropomorphisms. In reality, hormonal birds are not agents of the anthropocentric heteropatriarchy. Despite *Love Bird* clearly not being a work of realism, this one piece of reality may be useful to keep in mind as you read.

*

The script itself came into existence almost by accident. In 2016, despite having no background in theatre, I applied for a residency with Melbourne dramaturgical initiative Lonely Company. The final question on their application simply asked 'what's on your mind?' and out spilled the seeds of *Love Bird*. Throughout the following year, Bridget Mackey showed me how to wrangle my wayward ideas into dramatic scenes, and most importantly, she taught me how to create space within the text for creative collaboration.

During these mentorship sessions, I told Bridget that *Love Bird* was an exploration into how some children who are conditioned as female come to experience sexual development under the patriarchy. I explained to her

Introduction by the Author

how my play was about what happens when the innocence of a child meets with the innocence of an animal and how these interactions become contorted when filtered through the gaze of world-weary adults. As I was yet to learn, authorial intent is a strange and slippery thing—a solitary writer who brings their work into the collaborative sphere of live theatre is truly in for a baptism by fire.

I panicked when my Expression of Interest for The Butterfly Club was successful. I had no idea how theatre actually got made. Who could possibly be mad enough to want to handle the logistics of such a nightmare? Then I had a flashback: in 2016 I met Jessica To on the set of a dating show—we were assistants, not contestants—and she had handed me her business card with the title 'producer' embossed. Two years later, that card remained deep in my wallet. I sent Jess an email, we met for coffee, she introduced me to the brilliant director Phoebe Anne Taylor, and in this meeting the show was truly born.

We began rehearsals in November 2017, right after Tarana Burke's 'Me Too' movement found global recognition. While the text felt more relevant in its wake, it also felt more dangerous. Would actors feel safe playing these roles? How would audiences feel watching a comedy that wades through the highly conductive waters of child sexual development? How would they respond to jokes about paedophile parrots and rape-able ducks? Would they boo? Would they simply walk out?

We opened the show to a full house on January 30, 2018, and the seating banks continued to buzz throughout our debut season. The responses to the work were as diverse as the audience. People laughed in places we didn't expect, one audience member gleefully shouted 'No! Stop!' at a climactic moment, while others vocalised their experience through gasps and sobs. The season was well attended and well-reviewed except for a few quibbles about the claustrophobic set (fitting five actors onto The Butterfly Club's stage is no mean feat) and some concerns that, too faint-hearted, we'd leaned into the territory of sketch comedy.

In October of the same year, we staged an encore season at La Mama, Trades Hall. This time we had a longer timeslot, a bigger stage and emboldened hearts. We pushed the work further, teased out its dark undercurrents and left the audience to sit in some of the more poignant moments. *Love Bird 2.0* was more divisive, with one reviewer declaring it 'a very dangerous work'—but I suppose this will make good marketing copy for future seasons.

*

Introduction by the Author

As I watch Love Bird enter its new life, I am both anxious and thrilled by its preservation as a published work. The play will now be given the chance to age and interpretations may change radically overtime. For one thing, amidst the global pandemic, Joan's obsession with Dettol no longer seems such a foible. In the current moment, with fresh memory of our theatres darkened and empty, my greatest hope for this work is that it may one day again be part of that ephemeral magic of live bodies on and before a stage.

Georgie Harriss

Production History

Love Bird premiered at The Butterfly Club in Melbourne, on January 30, 2018. It was directed by **Phoebe Anne Taylor** and produced by **Jessica To**. The costume design was by **Jason Chalmers**, the sound design and music composition was by **Steve Carnell** and the puppets were designed and constructed by **Andrew Lucas**. The production was stage managed and assistant stage managed by **Jaklene Vukasinovic** and **Georgia Willmott** respectively.

Original Cast

Franny	**Jessica Martin**
Prince Ping Pong	**John Marc Desengano**
Joan	**Beth Liston**
Richard	**Matt Tester**
Bill/Ugboot/Boy	**Brendan McFarlane**

Love Bird

Georgie Harriss

Act 1

Scene 1

On the right side of the stage is a pillow fort decorated with fairy lights and birthday balloons. A young girl—FRANNY—sits and plays with her doll and teddy. On the other side of the stage is a small living room setup that could also be a bedroom.
Through the sheet Franny's parents—JOAN and RICHARD—can be heard arguing.

FRANNY   Today you get married Teddy. But you're not allowed to see the bride in her dress.

Franny shoves Teddy under a pillow. She wraps her doll in toilet paper.

RICHARD   I'm just saying, McDonalds two nights in a row? I don't think it's a good habit to be getting her into…

JOAN   It's her birthday!

RICHARD   But yesterday?

JOAN   I was a bit busy blowing up these fucking balloons. You could've cooked.

RICHARD   You know I can't cook. You're a genius.

Richard kisses Joan on the cheek.

JOAN   Bullshit Richard, steam some fucking carrots. Besides, Franny knows about your Dorito drawer. You can't have a double standard like that.

RICHARD   That's different.

JOAN   Because you're a heart attack waiting to happen?

RICHARD   When I was her age I was skinny as a rake. These are her formative years.

JOAN   And I don't want to give her a fucking eating disorder.

RICHARD   Neither do I, Joan. But childhood obesity, it creeps up on you. And then it's a lifelong struggle.

JOAN   Life is lifelong fucking struggle. We're talking about two fucking Happy Meals on her birthday weekend. She's a perfectly healthy girl.

Beat.

RICHARD   I think she should join a netball team.

JOAN   "Here if you need, here if you need". What kind of submissive fucking bullshit is that?

RICHARD   You've gotta be kidding.

JOAN   Men don't play netball.

RICHARD   You think she's better off playing a boy's sport? Some girls her age are as sporty as boys. Franny's just not…

JOAN   Then why make her do something she's bad at?

RICHARD   It's character-building. She should be running around having fun, getting some exercise.

JOAN   Leave her alone. You'll scar her for life.

RICHARD   It's the kids who'll scar her for life. And these are her…

JOAN   Formative years.

Knock Knock.

RICHARD   That'll be Bill.

Joan goes up to the pillow fort and parts the sheet.

JOAN   Franny, Dad's friend Bill is here with your birthday present.

Franny runs out and answers the door. Joan picks up the doll, toilet paper unravelling.

Bill enters carrying a cage covered with a sheet. He wears khaki and carries binoculars—looks like the binoculars aren't just for birdwatching. He puts the cage down and gives Franny's hair a ruffle. He shakes Richard's hand.

RICHARD   How you going, mate?

BILL   Not bad, not bad. We still on for next weekend?

RICHARD   You betcha, really think we'll catch a glimpse?

BILL   I'm telling ya, the place is teeming with them.

Joan enters with three beers.

JOAN   Next weekend?

BILL   Richard and I've got a date with some hot birds.

RICHARD   Powerful owls. Apparently they're nesting at the top of the ridge.

Bill kisses Joan on the cheek.

Act 1 *Scene 1*

FRANNY   How come Daddy got a handshake, Mummy got a kiss and I got scruffled?

RICHARD   It's good manners, Possum. Like please and thank you. Speaking of which, have you thanked Bill for your present?

BILL   She should find out what it is before she thanks me Rich, what if she hates it?

RICHARD   I'd still expect her to say thank you.

BILL   I bought you a selection.

JOAN   Brought.

Richard elbows Joan.

JOAN   Formative years.

Bill whips off the sheet to reveal three bird puppets—two grey scraggly ones, one brightly coloured. Franny inspects.

FRANNY   I want the ugliest one. Because one day it'll be the most beautiful. Just like me.

JOAN   We just read The Ugly Duckling.

BILL   Ohhh. Nah love. They're not babies, just females. Grey and scraggly 'til the day they die. You see with birds, girls are the ugly buggers, and men are the beauties.

FRANNY   So girls are the hunters?

BILL   Nope.

FRANNY   The best singers?

BILL   Nup.

FRANNY   So they're just grey?

JOAN   But do females make better pets?

FRANNY   I don't want a crappy grey one!

JOAN   Language!

BILL   To be honest, the only people who buy the womenfolk are breeders. Parrots are meant to be colourful; the grey scragglies are sort of a means to an end. You know what they say? You can't make an omelette without cracking a few female reproductive organs.

Silence.

BILL   A male will bond more closely with her.

RICHARD   Sounds like a no-brainer.

Act 1   Scene 1

JOAN   He sure does.
BILL   Sorry?
JOAN   We've got the cage, what else do we need?
BILL   You're all set. But stay away from those little mirrors they sell in pet shops. Don't want him to get confused thinking it's another bird. In the first few months Franny will have a hard time competing with the genuine article.
JOAN   And after a few months?
BILL   He won't remember what a bird is.
RICHARD   He'll think he's a person?
BILL   He'll practically be a person. (*BEAT*) Buy him a bell instead. Remember those first few months are...
JOAN & RICHARD
                Formative.

BILL GRABS THE BIRD PUPPET OUT OF ONE CAGE AND HANDS IT TO FRANNY.

BILL   He'll be head over heels for you in no time, Sweetheart.

FRANNY LOOKS AT IT DISAPPOINTED AND CONFUSED. RICHARD NUDGES HER.

FRANNY   Thank you.
BILL   Good girl. Better get these ladies back to the production line.

BILL WINKS, PICKS UP THE CAGE AND EXITS. RICHARD SITS DOWN AND PULLS FRANNY ONTO HIS LAP.

RICHARD   Do you know what you're going to call him, Possum?
FRANNY   He's a prince.
RICHARD   Is he now?
FRANNY   That's his crown.
RICHARD   So His Majesty's name is Prince?
FRANNY   No. Prince Ping Pong.
RICHARD   Makes sense. Well then Prince Ping Pong, I hope you're good enough for my princess.
FRANNY   One day I'm going to marry a real prince.
RICHARD   Maybe if you kiss Ping Pong, he'll turn into a real prince.
JOAN   Don't you kiss that bird Franny, you'll get a disease.
RICHARD   Your mother's right. Kissing can make you sick.
FRANNY   Is that why the boys get detention for playing kiss-chasey?

JOAN	Yep. Meningococcal. They sent out a warning in the school newsletter.
FRANNY	I don't like kiss-chasey anyway, I'm not fast enough.
RICHARD	Would you like to join a netball team, Possum? You might get a bit faster.
JOAN	Richard! They shouldn't be chasing her in the first place. Not if she doesn't want to play.
FRANNY	I might want to play if the others didn't make fun of me. The boys only like chasing the faster girls.
RICHARD	Boys like a challenge. You just don't have the competitive spirit yet.
JOAN	No, no, no. Boys are silly. And kissing is yucky.
FRANNY	I won't have time anyway. I'll be too busy with Prince Ping Pong.
JOAN	That's right. Looking after a pet is a big responsibility. He's reliant on you for everything: food, water, love and attention.

FRANNY CROSSES HER ARMS.

FRANNY	I look after Dolly and Teddy all by myself.

FRANNY WHIPS DOLLY CLOSE TO HER CHEST, WHACKING HER HEAD.

JOAN	But you understand that Dolly is a toy? She doesn't feel things.
FRANNY	She does too! She loves me. And she's going to marry Teddy. You have to love someone to do that!
JOAN	Then why did you ask for a pet?
FRANNY	I want Ping Pong to love me all on his own.
RICHARD	It'll take some time Franny; he might not fall in love overnight.
JOAN	But if you go to sleep now, the sooner you can wake up and start training him.

FRANNY CRAWLS INTO HER PILLOW FORT. RICHARD CARRIES THE CAGE IN AFTER HER.

RICHARD	Goodnight Princess.
FRANNY	Goodnight Prince Ping Pong.

RICHARD PUTS A SHEET OVER THE CAGE. SWITCHES OFF LIGHT.

Scene 2

Ping Pong squawks

A nightlight switches on and illuminates Ping Pong's shadow. Franny pokes the bird with Dolly's arm. Ping squawks louder.

FRANNY   What is it Prince Ping Pong?

Squawk

FRANNY   Are you thirsty?

Franny pours a bit of juice box over him. He squawks and flaps.

FRANNY   Hungry?

Franny pulls a packet of Doritos out from under her bed. She shooshes him.

FRANNY   Don't tell.

Ping Pong rejects the chip. Franny eats it loudly.

FRANNY   (*with her mouth full*) Are you lonely?

Ping stops.

FRANNY   It's okay to be lonely. That's what mum said to Aunty Jane on the phone. She said having a husband and child won't make it go away. The real cure is knowing yourself. Then I walked in and she gave me a cuddle. (*Beat*) Do you want to be the priest for Teddy and Dolly's wedding?

Franny puts a white scrunchie around his neck. He squawks louder.

Lights dim on Franny as a reading light illuminates Joan and Richard's bed. A pile of bird books sit on Richard's bedside table.

JOAN   It's like having a fucking baby in the house again.

RICHARD   So the best thing that ever happened to us. Minus all your post-natal... Stuff.

JOAN   Stuff? That's cute. God must be a real fucking misogynist to follow childbirth with that pit of despair—Will that bird ever shut up!

RICHARD   He can't be that bad if it ended in Franny.

JOAN   Ended?

RICHARD   You know what I mean.

JOAN   Don't act like you love her more than I do. I love her to fucking pieces. (*Beat*) You know they live for 20 years?

Act 1　　　　　　　　　　　　　　　　　　　　　　　　　　　　Scene 2

RICHARD　　　They do not.

PAUSE.

RICHARD　　　That would make Franny 28 when it dies.

RICHARD PICKS UP THE COCKATIEL MANUAL.

JOAN　　　It'll make me 55. You'll be 56. Franny will have flown the nest and we'll be left in this empty house with a geriatric fucking cockatiel. I want to travel.

RICHARD　　　"Life expectancy 15-20 years". I wish Bill had mentioned that… Maybe it'll get cancer or something.

JOAN　　　Maybe you will.

RICHARD　　　I was joking.

JOAN　　　So was I. But you might. I might.

SQUAWKING STARTS AGAIN.

JOAN　　　20 fucking years. I can't concentrate.

JOAN PULLS A VIBRATING EGG FROM UNDER THE COVERS AND HANDS IT TO RICHARD. HE INSPECTS IT.

JOAN WALKS OVER AND POKES HER HEAD INTO THE PILLOW FORT. FRANNY IS TIPPING THE LEFTOVER DORITOS OVER PING PONG. JOAN PICKS UP THE DORITO PACKET.

JOAN　　　Where did you get these? Richard!

RICHARD PUTS THE VIBRATING EGG IN HIS DORITO DRAWER. PULLS OUT EMPTY PACKETS, CONFUSED.

FRANNY　　　I'm not eating them. It's confetti.

JOAN　　　Why have you put that thing around Ping's neck?

FRANNY　　　Teddy and Dolly need a priest for their wedding.

JOAN　　　They're inanimate objects Fran, they don't need anything. But Ping needs respect.

FRANNY　　　I don't think he likes them.

JOAN　　　People like different things.

FRANNY　　　What if he doesn't like me?

JOAN　　　He will.

FRANNY　　　How do you know?

PAUSE.

JOAN　　　Instincts.

FRANNY　　　What's instincts?

Act 1   Scene 2

JOAN   It's sort of knowing something that you've never been taught. They help animals survive in the wild.

FRANNY   Do I have instincts?

JOAN   Yep.

FRANNY   Does Ping Pong have instincts?

JOAN   Definitely.

FRANNY   And you have instincts?

JOAN   Everyone does.

FRANNY   And yours say he'll love me?

JOAN   Not mine, his. Ping Pong will rely on you to feed him, make sure he has fresh water and to keep him company. His instincts will tell him to love you to bits.

FRANNY   So love is an instinct?

JOAN   … I'll have a think.

FRANNY   I wish his instincts were working now.

JOAN   Give it time. If you can't sleep, why don't you read him one of your school readers?

FRANNY   That's not fun.

JOAN   Not everything in life is fun. I want lights off in half an hour.

JOAN RETURNS TO BED.

JOAN   Do you think love's instinctive or learned?

RICHARD   I can google it?

FRANNY   Do you want to hear a story? I'm getting good at reading. I'm not the best though. Zoe in my class can read so well her big sister gave her all her old Dolly magazines.

PING PONG COCKS HIS HEAD.

FRANNY   It's about dolls I guess. I like dolls but I know you don't. So I've picked one about giraffes.

Scene 3

PING PONG SQUAWKS. FRANNY ENTERS, IN SCHOOL UNIFORM.
SHE FEEDS PING. HE TWEETS. SHE CROUCHES AND WHISTLES. PING STRUTS AND MAKES AFFECTIONATE NOISES. FRANNY OPENS THE CAGE. HE HOPS ONTO HER HAND.

FRANNY   Hi Ping Pong. Do you want to play with me?!

FRANNY   (*AS PING PONG*) Of course I do Franny. I love you.

FRANNY   I love you too Ping.

PING FLAPS HIS WINGS AND BOBS HIS HEAD. FRANNY RUBS HER NOSE AGAINST HIS BEAK. PING'S CREST BECOMES ERECT. HE DANCES FROM SIDE TO SIDE. IT BECOMES MORE VIGOROUS, MORE LIKE GRINDING.

FRANNY   That tickles.

THE BIRD RUBS ITS BOTTOM SIDE-TO-SIDE ON FRANNY'S HAND. SHE GIGGLES.

FRANNY   That's the silliest dance. Can you teach me?

FRANNY DANCES WITH PING PONG. HE STOPS ABRUPTLY. SATISFIED, HE PUFFS OUT HIS FEATHERS, HOPS OFF HER HAND AND EATS A SUNFLOWER SEED.

FRANNY   But I wasn't finished.

FRANNY LOOKS DOWN AT HER HANDS.

FRANNY   You're all sticky?

FRANNY SNIFFS HER HAND. SHRUGS. WIPES IT ON HER DRESS.

JINGLING KEYS, JOAN ENTERS AND SITS DOWN. FRANNY HOPS ON HER LAP.

JOAN   Hi Possum.

FRANNY   Mum, guess what! Ping Pong just hopped on my hand.

JOAN   That's nice.

FRANNY   And he did the silliest dance.

JOAN LOOKS THROUGH FRANNY'S HAIR.

JOAN   Have any of the kids at school been scratching their heads?

FRANNY SHAKES HER HEAD. JOAN RUMMAGES IN HER HAIR.

JOAN   It'd be a shame if we had to shave off all your pretty hair.

FRANNY SHAKES HER HEAD AND THEN HER WHOLE BODY. SHE DOES THE DANCE FROM BEFORE, RUBBING FIRMLY AGAINST JOAN'S LAP. SHE IS ENJOYING IT.

JOAN LAUGHS BUT SLOWLY GROWS CONCERNED.

Act 1	Scene 4

JOAN	What are you doing? Are you itchy down there? I told you, you have to change your underwear every single day.

PAUSE.

JOAN	Have you been wiping from front to back?

PAUSE.

JOAN	You haven't been sitting on the cold cement at school?
FRANNY	It's what baby birds do with their mothers. It's Ping Pong's silly dance. It was so cute! But it was weird and it made my hands a bit sticky.

FRANNY THRUSTS HER HAND IN JOAN'S FACE

FRANNY	See!
JOAN	Oh my God Franny, that's disgusting! Go wash your hands right now!

FRANNY RUNS OFF DISTRESSED. JOAN CARRIES THE CAGE OUT OF THE PILLOW FORT AND INTO HER OWN BEDROOM. SHE POPS A PANADOL AND LIES DOWN.

JOAN	Don't forget the Dettol!

Scene 4

JOAN WAKES UP. A MAN IN A PARROT SUIT LIES NEXT TO HER. SHE HITS HIM WITH A PILLOW BUT HE USES THE PUPPET AS A SHIELD.

JOAN	You're an animal!

THE MAN COCKS HIS HEAD. JOAN PULLS A BLANKET OFF THE EDGE OF THE FORT AND THROWS IT OVER HIM. HE SQUAWKS.

RICHARD ENTERS, EARS COVERED.

RICHARD	What's his problem?
JOAN	He's a sexual deviant, that's what his problem is.
RICHARD	With the racket he's making, the neighbours will call the RSPCA.
JOAN	They should call child services.
RICHARD	Why? Where's Franny?
JOAN	In the bathroom. That bird Bill gave us, it used Franny's hand as a fucking… fucking masturbatory apparatus!

RICHARD PROCESSES.

RICHARD	Right.

Act 1 Scene 4

HE FIGHTS LAUGHTER.

JOAN   You think it's funny? The hilarious paedophile parrot.

THE PUPPET TWEETS INNOCENTLY. RICHARD IGNORES THE MAN.

RICHARD   It's a bird in heat Joan, he's a slave to his instincts.

JOAN   So he's just primal enough to ejaculate all over our daughter, but not primal enough to recognise she's a different fucking species?

RICHARD   Joan. It's a bird. You can't try and convict.

JOAN   Why not?

RICHARD   It's called "mens rea" for a reason.

RICHARD LAUGHS AT HIS OWN JOKE.

JOAN   It's got mens rea coming out its dick!

RICHARD   Calm down.

JOAN   I want it gone. Ring up Bill, get him to take it away.

RICHARD   That'd be pretty rude after he came all this way. Franny has no idea it was sexual. What she doesn't know…

JOAN   You know how I found out? She started grinding her vagina on my lap.

RICHARD   Jesus. Don't talk about her (*WHISPERING*) vagina like that. She's only eight.

JOAN   I fucking know Richard.

FRANNY ENTERS, TEARY-EYED.

FRANNY   I hate Dettol, it stinks. What did I do wrong?

JOAN   You didn't do anything wrong. But animals are full of germs, you have to wash your hands every time you… touch them. Or you might get sick.

FRANNY CLOCKS THE CAGE.

FRANNY   Why have you taken Ping Pong away?

RICHARD   Your Mum and I are jealous, we want to spend time with him too.

JOAN   Franny, I need you to listen. You can't rub yourself against Mummy like that. Or against anyone else. Ever. It's not allowed.

FRANNY   But it's what birds do.

JOAN   Not any more they don't.

Love Bird

Act 1   Scene 4

FRANNY   Why?
JOAN   Ping Pong did that dance because he thinks you're very special.
RICHARD   What are you doing Joan?
JOAN   Telling her what she needs to know.
FRANNY   Being special is good.
RICHARD   I don't think she needs to…
JOAN   Do you know where babies come from?
RICHARD   Okay, so you're doing this…
FRANNY   From inside a mum's belly.
JOAN   Do you know how they get inside?

FRANNY SHAKES HER HEAD.

JOAN   When a man thinks a mummy is very special, they do a silly dance together and that dance puts a baby inside her. That was what Ping Pong was doing.
FRANNY   He was trying to put a baby inside me?
RICHARD   Good, excellent.
JOAN   Sort of.
FRANNY   I'm his mum! I think you're a bit wrong… Unless, did I make you pregnant?
JOAN   (*TO RICHARD*) Do you want to help me here?

RICHARD LOOKS AT THE PUPPET.

RICHARD   I guess he didn't turn into a real prince…

THE BIRD MAN IS OFFENDED.

FRANNY   I'm not his mum anymore? I'm his wife!
JOAN   No.
RICHARD   You should have called him King Oedipus instead.
FRANNY   King eat-a-puss?

JOAN CRACKS AND LAUGHS.

Scene 5

FRANNY IS ASLEEP IN HER PILLOW FORT. IT'S MORE SPARSE THAN BEFORE.
THE BIRD MAN SNORES.
FRANNY SHAKES THE CAGE GENTLY AND WAKES HIM. HE SQUAWKS, THEN TWEETS.

FRANNY   I thought I was going to marry a real prince. But I guess we're married now. Maybe if we kiss properly you'll turn into a real prince? I don't really believe in magic, I'm too smart. But Mum said a dance puts babies inside you, and she's pretty smart…

FRANNY LEANS IN AND KISSES THE MAN ON THE BEAK. THE MAN'S CREST GOES ERECT.

FRANNY   Didn't work.

RICHARD ENTERS. FRANNY JUMPS BACK AND TRIES TO LOOK INNOCENT.

RICHARD   Whatcha up to Possum?

FRANNY   Ping tried to put babies inside me so we're getting married.

RICHARD   And you didn't invite your own mother?

FRANNY   I don't think she likes Ping very much.

RICHARD   Nobody likes their in-laws Franny. She probably thinks you're too young to be tied down by a man.

FRANNY   Tied down? Why would…

RICHARD   Never mind. In real weddings, your father gives you away.

FRANNY   (*UPSET*) Don't you want me anymore?

RICHARD   Of course I want you, Darling.

FRANNY   Then why would you give me away?

RICHARD   It's like… remember that time you really wanted to keep that Safari Barbie? But you had to give it to your friend Josie as a birthday present?

FRANNY   It was my birthday.

RICHARD   But this is a wedding. And to be fair, Ping was already given to you as your birthday present.

FRANNY   So he's my birthday present? And I'm his wedding present?

RICHARD	Let's not dwell on that.
FRANNY	Ping Pong's father isn't here to give him away. I was his mother… But not anymore because of the silly dance.
RICHARD	It's okay Possum, boys don't get given away at weddings.
FRANNY	Why not?
RICHARD	Remember that time Aunty Jane gave you a Ken doll for Christmas? You cried.
FRANNY	Ken dolls suck.
RICHARD	Exactly. Now where were we?
FRANNY	(*IN A RAISED VOICE*) You were giving me away as a wedding present.
RICHARD	Shhh Sweetie, we really don't want to disturb your mother.

FRANNY HUMS THE WEDDING TUNE AND RICHARD WALKS HER TOWARDS THE CAGE. RICHARD HUGS FRANNY. PING SQUAWKS AND FLAPS.

FRANNY	Shhh Ping Pong! Why is he doing that? He doesn't want me either!
RICHARD	I think he's jealous.
FRANNY	But you haven't even given me away yet!

JOAN ENTERS, UNSEEN. SHE CARRIES A BIRD-SIZED MIRROR AND ATTACHES IT TO THE CAGE.

RICHARD	It's because he wants you all to himself. Like that time Josie started playing with your most favourite teddy and you got really upset? That's how Ping Pong is feeling right now.

JOAN MOUTHS ANGRILY AT RICHARD FROM BEHIND FRANNY'S BACK.

FRANNY	So you and I don't get to hug anymore because Ping Pong doesn't like it?
RICHARD	His Royal Highness is going to have to learn to share. Now you two go off to bed.
FRANNY	For our honeymoon?

FRANNY AND PARROT MAN HOLD HANDS.

RICHARD	Go to bed.
JOAN	What the fuck just happened?
RICHARD	We were just playing a game.
JOAN	It seeps in, it all seeps in.

Scene 6

FRANNY SITS IN BED WASHING HER HANDS WITH DETTOL. PARROT MAN LIES DOWN SMOKING A CIGARETTE.

FRANNY GOES TO EAT A DORITO BUT THE BAG IS EMPTY. SHE SNEAKS NEXT DOOR AND RUMMAGES THROUGH RICHARD'S DRAWER. SHE FINDS THE VIBRATING EGG AND READS IT.

FRANNY   Love egg?

FRANNY PUTS THE EGG ON THE GROUND THEN LOWERS HERSELF ON TOP.

FRANNY   It's not hatching. Sorry Ping. I think nobody taught Mum that magic isn't real.

THE PARROT MAN SHRUGS. FRANNY PICKS UP THE EGG. SHE ACCIDENTALLY HITS THE SWITCH.

FRANNY   (*WHISPERS*) Magic?

FRANNY SITS ON THE EGG AGAIN. SHE JUMPS UPS, ALARMED. SHE LOOKS DOWN AT HER CROTCH. SHE SITS BACK DOWN. SHE JUMPS BACK UP. SHE GOES OVER TO THE CAGE AND PULLS OUT THE MIRROR. SHE ANGLES THE MIRROR UNDER HER DRESS. SHE DOES A SHOULDER STAND ON THE BED, PULLS DOWN HER DRESS AND HOLDS THE MIRROR TO HER PRIVATES. SHE GIVES HERSELF A GENTLE PROD.

THE PARROT MAN WATCHES, FASCINATED.

RICHARD   Franny, are you ready…

RICHARD ENTERS. HE STOPS. COVERS HIS EYES.

RICHARD   Jesus. Oh God. Franny. Go to your roo… Stop.

FRANNY   It's okay Dad, I washed my hands.

RICHARD TURNS AWAY.

RICHARD   Wash them again, then… I don't know, go to the kitchen!

FRANNY   I'm sorry Dad.

RICHARD   It's okay. Have a Tim Tam or a Paddle Pop or something. Everything's fine.

FRANNY EXITS.

RICHARD CLOSES HIS EYES AND BREATHES. HE OPENS THEM AND SEES PARROT MAN FOR THE FIRST TIME.

RICHARD   This is your fault.

PARROT MAN SHRUGS.

Act 1   Scene 6

RICHARD GRABS HIS COLLAR AND SWINGS. PARROT MAN DUCKS, SHIELDING HIMSELF WITH THE PUPPET.

RICHARD   What am I doing? It's just a bird. It's just a bird.

PARROT MAN NODS.

RICHARD PULLS A SHEET OFF THE FORT AND THROWS IT OVER THE MAN.

JOAN ENTERS.

JOAN   Where's Franny.

RICHARD   Eating Tim Tams in the kitchen.

JOAN   (*SARCASTICALLY*) But these are her formative years?

RICHARD   I needed to calm her down.

JOAN   You're teaching her to comfort eat?

RICHARD   I just walked in to see if she was ready for dinner and she was… (*WHISPERING*) touching herself.

JOAN   She's eight.

RICHARD   I know what I saw Joan.

JOAN   Fuck. Fuck. It's natural isn't it? Fuck. Shit. Did you at least make her wash her hands before she started eating?

RICHARD   That's another thing, when I walked in the whole room already smelt of Dettol…

JOAN GLARES AT PARROT MAN. SHE LOOKS BACK AT RICHARD.

JOAN   What do you mean?

RICHARD   I don't know.

JOAN   You think the bird was on her hand… and then…

RICHARD   He looked pretty pleased with himself. Watching.

JOAN LOOKS DOWN ON THE FLOOR AND PICKS UP THE VIBRATING EGG. SHE HIDES IT BEHIND HER BACK. RICHARD SEES THE EMPTY DORITO PACKET AND HIDES IT BEHIND HIS.

JOAN   You always like to watch.

RICHARD   You. You're an adult. And you're so good at it.

JOAN   Animals. Both of you.

RICHARD   Can birds transmit… you know (whispering) sexually?

JOAN   Google it?

RICHARD   I don't want that on my search history.

JOAN   For fuck sake. Call Bill, I bet he knows all about it. He probably trained the bird as some kind of prank.

Act 1   Scene 6

RICHARD   This is a bit private. We don't want to seem ungrateful.

JOAN   Jesus Christ, we'll use my laptop. "Bird + sexually transmitted diseases".

JOAN TYPES.

JOAN   There's a video here called… "Drake ejaculates"?

RICHARD   Couldn't hurt right?

RICHARD AND JOAN SIT ON THE COUCH/BED WATCHING. PARROT MAN CREEPS BEHIND THEM AND LEANS OVER TO WATCH. THEIR EYES WIDEN. JOAN AND RICHARD FIDGET NERVOUSLY WITH WHAT'S IN THEIR HANDS. DORITOS RUSTLE IN RICHARD'S LAP, THE VIBRATOR SWITCHES ON IN JOAN'S. THEY FIND THEMSELVES HUDDLING CLOSER AND CLOSER TOGETHER UNTIL THE CLIMAX. THEY SIGH IN ORGASM-LIKE RELIEF.

JOAN   Oh my God.

RICHARD   Why is it shaped like that?

JOAN TYPES. CLICKS. READS.

JOAN   Says here forty percent of duck-sex is forced.

RICHARD   Do ducks really have the capacity for consent?

JOAN   "To avoid unwanted pregnancies, female ducks evolved to have cryptic, spiralling vaginas".

RICHARD   Cryptic?

JOAN   And males evolved to have stronger, corkscrew-shaped penises. Apparently it's called sexually antagonistic coevolution. Fuck. Evolution is a fucking cunt.

RICHARD   A cryptic cunt.

JOAN   Don't use the word cunt like that. Like it actually means vagina.

RICHARD   We can't judge ducks by our moral standards. It's survival of the fittest.

JOAN   But the most rape-able ducks—the ones who can't defend themselves—are also most likely to get pregnant and reproduce, so how are they the fittest?

RICHARD   I guess they're not. But maybe their genes are more easily dominated by the strong, corkscrew penis genes? They don't dilute the pool.

JOAN   Her body's not enough, they've gotta fuck her genes too? God, does that make our Franny the most… rape-able duck?

RICHARD   … Ping's a cockatiel not a duck. Google cockatiel sex.

Joan thrusts the laptop towards Richard.

JOAN   I knew I fucking hated birds. I even got the little creep a mirror so he could fall in love with himself—fuck his reflection with his freak corkscrew dick—Where's it gone?

RICHARD   She was using it to…

JOAN   … look at her vagina. Her dad caught her looking at her vagina in a bird-mirror, and now she's banished to the kitchen eating Tim Tams. Excellent. Good job.

RICHARD   Do you think maybe this will all just… blow over?

Joan laughs. Richard joins in. Mild to extreme hysteria ensues.

Scene 7

Franny stomps around in her fort, feathers strewn everywhere. Many pillows and sheets have disappeared. Parrot Man bashes his head against his bell in imitation.

The phones rings. Joan races in to answer it. Parrot Man tries to imitate the ring.

JOAN   Hello? Oh yes hi. She did seem a bit upset, but she's been going through a difficult time. I'm so sorry, that is awkward. I'm sure they weren't traumatised. They're going to find out sooner or—Okay look, just tell the parents that they have to deal with this kind of thing. I said I was sorry, but quite frankly, I'm not. And Franny doesn't even want to be allowed to take the pet canary home. You can't even control a bunch of eight year olds! As if you can control my tone!

She slams the phone down. Richard enters.

RICHARD   Was that your father?

JOAN   School office. During show and tell, Franny told the class about the birds and the bees. The focus being on one bird in particular.

RICHARD   No.

JOAN   Some of the parents got very upset. Turns out they wanted to decide if, and under what circumstances, they taught their children about bestiality.

RICHARD	What's the damage?
JOAN	For one, she's not allowed to take home the class canary anymore—thank fucking God—I want to save the avian three-way until she's at least nine and a half.

JOAN GETS VISIBLY UPSET.

JOAN	Fuck Richard, all of the other kids are calling her Mrs Big Bird. She was having a hard enough time making friends as it is.
RICHARD	I'm sorry.
JOAN	(*FIGHTING TEARS*) Really? You don't find it hilarious that our daughter's being slut-shamed by the entire second-grade because she let a bird fuck her hand?
RICHARD	No, I'm taking this seriously. I am. But I'm not going to blame an innocent animal.
JOAN	An innocent animal with a rape instinct.
RICHARD	He's not a duck. He's a cockatiel.
JOAN	Same fucking difference.
RICHARD	Poor Franny, but I'm sorry Joan, you can't just blame the bird.
JOAN	This never would have happened if you'd made her pick one of the grey, scraggly ones.
RICHARD	Oh of course this absurd, incredibly unpredictable situation is my fault. No wait, not my fault, it's masculinity's fault. So what, you'll just teach Franny that all men are evil?
JOAN	Grow the fuck up Richard. This isn't about blame; it's about protecting our fucking daughter.
RICHARD	Okay fine. What should we do, lock him up?
JOAN	How about we send him back to Bill's farm?
RICHARD	We don't want to seem ungrateful, this isn't Bill's fault. Now bear with me, but could we sneak some rat pellets into his bird seed?
JOAN	What? What about "it's an innocent animal"?
RICHARD	That was more of a philosophical argument.
JOAN	So your philosophical solution is to take him out?
RICHARD	As I've been saying all along, it's just a bird.

JOAN	Franny thinks he's her "husband".
RICHARD	I was brainstorming. Come to think of it, I've seen Franny eat some of that bird seed.
JOAN	That's disgusting.
RICHARD	It's probably healthier than those muesli bars you pack in her lunchbox.
JOAN	Shut up Richard.

Scene 8

RICHARD, JOAN AND FRANNY SIT ON THE COUCH. PARROT MAN SITS IN A CAGE BEFORE THEM. ON TRIAL. THERE IS A PLATE OF TIM TAMS IN FRONT OF FRANNY.

RICHARD	Go ahead, Sweetie.

FRANNY LOOKS AT THEM. SHE TAKES ONE AND NIBBLES IT.

JOAN	Do you want to talk about how you're feeling Franny?

SHE SHAKES HER HEAD.

RICHARD	You haven't done anything wrong Possum.
FRANNY	I think I did do something wrong. The other kids laugh every time I'm near them. They whisper. Whenever I try and play with them at lunchtime they run away. I try to chase them but I'm too slow.
JOAN	Why do you think that is?
FRANNY	They think I'm weird. They think Prince Ping Pong is weird too. They just don't understand, they're not very mature.
JOAN	Do you sit by yourself?
FRANNY	I go to the liberry.
JOAN	Library.
FRANNY	Library. It has the best books. There's one about Australian parrots that's my favourite. There's a picture of Ping in it. It looks exactly the same. So beautiful.

BOTH THE PARENTS TURN SHARPLY AND GLARE AT PING PONG. HE SHRUGS.

RICHARD	We need to talk about Ping. Your mum and I think he's a bad influence.
FRANNY	He's my best friend.

Act 1   *Scene 8*

RICHARD	You need real friends, Possum. Other children. That's why we've enrolled you in another school.
JOAN	We think you'll really like it there.
FRANNY	Nobody will want to be my friend.
JOAN	Everyone will want to be your friend Franny, you're wonderful!
FRANNY	Do they have a class canary?
JOAN	No.
RICHARD	Wouldn't you like having human friends?
FRANNY	They're not very nice.

KNOCK KNOCK.

RICHARD	We've decided Ping Pong should have a friend too. A bird friend.

BILL ENTERS WITH A SHEET-COVERED CAGE. HE KISSES JOAN ON THE CHEEK.

BILL	Joan, looking gorgeous as always. Hi Princess.

BILL PUTS DOWN THE CAGE. HE SHAKES RICHARD'S HAND.

BILL	How are ya, mate?
RICHARD	Alright, yourself?
BILL	Yeah not bad, not bad. Now sounds to me like you've really fallen in love with the old bugger. Knew it would happen. They're bloody magical.

RICHARD AND JOAN SHARE A LOOK.

RICHARD	Franny, do you want to go put the kettle on for Bill?

FRANNY EXITS.

RICHARD	(*EMBARRASSED*) Thing is Bill, the bird's become very attached…
BILL	What's the point of an indifferent pet?
JOAN	I never wanted a pet in the first place.
BILL	What's a pet to look after when you have a child?
RICHARD	We do have a child, Bill. And the bird you sold us has been…
JOAN	Using her as a sex toy.

BILL STOPS FOR A MOMENT. BURSTS INTO LAUGHTER.

BILL	That's what you meant by "attached"? Relax, that kind of thing is very common. Just part of life really. You can't

Love Bird

Act 1   Scene 8

	have your cake, and expect it not to cum on your shoulder every now and then.
RICHARD	I really wish you'd warned me that this sort of thing might happen.
BILL	You brought a wild animal for the sole purpose of loving your daughter.
JOAN	Bought!
BILL	What'd you expect? Lilo and Stitch?
JOAN	Yes!
BILL	I don't know what to tell ya. Birds will be birds, no matter how domesticated they are. Didn't think I needed to spell the facts of life out for you.
JOAN	Well it's really fucked us up Bill.
BILL	I'll say. What do you want me to do about it?
JOAN	Franny's very attached, we don't want to get rid of him. We just want to divert his attention. We've already tried the mirror.
BILL	You want to sacrifice a grey scraggly to the beast?
JOAN	A means to an end, right?
BILL	It's not that simple, cockatiels are emotionally complex creatures.
RICHARD	Who just happen to like rubbing their dicks all over children of another species?

FRANNY ENTERS, UNSEEN.

BILL	Ducks have dicks, mate. Cockatiels have cloacas.
FRANNY	What's a cloaca?

BILL PULLS THE SHEET OFF THE CAGE. IT CONTAINS TWO GREY, SCRAGGLY BIRDS.

BILL	Franny! Your Mum and Dad want you to pick out Ping's new friend.
FRANNY	These ones are boring. Can't he have another boy to play with?
BILL	Boys get jealous and fight. You don't want Ping Pong to get hurt do you?

FRANNY SHAKES HER HEAD.

BILL	He'll be much happier with one of these ugly ducklings.

JOAN	They do look very young… How old are they?
BILL	Fledglings. But don't worry, they'll be ready for your purposes in no time.
FRANNY	That one there. It's so teensy and fluffy.

BILL PULLS ONE OUT OF THE CAGE. RICHARD NUDGES FRANNY.

FRANNY	Thank you.
BILL	Good girl.
RICHARD	See you Monday? I've got a hot lead on a night parrot.
BILL	The holy grail? You're crazy, mate.

BILL EXITS.

JOAN	What will you call Ping's new friend?
FRANNY	Ugboot.
RICHARD	She is a bit plain.
FRANNY	She's fluffy like an ugboot.
JOAN	Okay Franny, say goodnight to Ping Pong and his new friend… Ugboot.

JOAN AND RICHARD EXIT.

FRANNY	Sweet dreams Prince Ping Pong. Goodnight Ugboot. I hope you like your new home.

PING PONG AND UGBOOT SIT OPPOSITE SIDES OF THE CAGE.

FRANNY THROWS THE SHEET OVER THEM AND RETURNS TO THE PILLOW FORT.

ACT 2

Scene 1

PING PONG AND UGBOOT ARE CENTRE STAGE. PING LOOKS FOR HUMANS. PACES.

UGBOOT TWEETS. PING PONG SQUAWKS. UGBOOT SQUAWKS. NO-ONE COMES.

PING BEGINS TO IMITATE THE PHONE RING. JOAN ENTERS. SHE ANSWERS THE PHONE. NOTHING.

RICHARD ENTERS, AGITATED.

RICHARD	Who was that?
JOAN	Nobody.
RICHARD	It only rang three times; who gives up by the third ring?
JOAN	Maybe they realised it was the wrong number?
RICHARD	Or they just like wasting peoples' time. Pathetic.
JOAN	What's your problem?
RICHARD	I'm waiting for a call. An important one.
JOAN	About what?
RICHARD	It's not that important. I probably won't get it.
JOAN	I'm sure an important call will last longer than two rings.

RICHARD NODS. JOAN HUGS HIM.

JOAN	They'd stay on the line to leave a message.

THEY BOTH SIGH.

JOAN	Do you think Ping likes Ugboot?
RICHARD	What's not to like? She's a bird, he's also a bird. They have so much in common.
JOAN	I hope she's comfortable.

PAUSE.

JOAN	Franny will be home soon.

JOAN EXITS.

RICHARD SITS DOWN WITH HIS LAPTOP.

ACT 2　　　　　　　　　　　　　　　　　　　　　　　　　　　　*Scene 1*

UGBOOT TRIES TO NUZZLE PING PONG'S PUPPET. PARROT MAN BASHES HIS BEAK AGAINST THE CAGE. NO RESPONSE FROM RICHARD. PARROT MAN SQUAWKS VIOLENTLY. UGBOOT JOINS IN.

RICHARD　　　What is your problem?

RICHARD THROWS A SHEET OVER THE CAGE.

RICHARD　　　Go to sleep.

THE PHONES RINGS. RICHARD LUNGES TOWARDS IT.

RICHARD　　　Hello, Richard McGrath speaking.

PAUSE.

RICHARD　　　Hello? Hello? Richard here. Hello!

RICHARD INSPECTS THE PHONE. THE RINGING STARTS AGAIN. IT'S NOT COMING FROM THE PHONE. RICHARD HANGS UP. HE WALKS AROUND THE ROOM LOOKING FOR THE SOURCE OF THE SOUND. HE WALKS TOWARDS THE CAGE AND WHIPS OFF THE SHEET.

RICHARD　　　You little bastards.

FRANNY ENTERS. PARROT MAN PERKS UP.

RICHARD　　　Hi Darling, how was school?

FRANNY　　　Boring.

RICHARD　　　Make any friends?

FRANNY　　　No.

RICHARD　　　I'm sorry, Possum.

FRANNY　　　It's okay, at least I have Prince Ping Pong. He loves me.

RICHARD　　　Yes, yes he does. Possum I don't want you to get upset if he starts paying more attention to Ugboot.

FRANNY　　　Ugboot's just a baby.

RICHARD　　　Birds mature a lot faster than people.

FRANNY　　　I am mature! I'm more mature than Ugboot!

RICHARD　　　I just mean you're not finished growing yet.

FRANNY　　　I'm bigger than she is!

RICHARD　　　You won't lay eggs Franny. Not now, not ever. Ugboot will.

FRANNY　　　So he'll stop loving me, because I can't lay eggs?

PAUSE.

FRANNY　　　How does he know? Can he see inside me? Can he see something wrong?

ACT 2　　　　　　　　　　　　　　　　　　　　　　　　Scene 1

RICHARD　　　Sort of. Not wrong, Possum. Just... different.

FRANNY　　　... You're wrong. Ping Pong and I got married! You gave me away.

RICHARD　　　What if I want you back?

FRANNY　　　I guess you'd have to ask.

RICHARD　　　Can I please have you back?

FRANNY　　　Not me, him.

RICHARD LAUGHS AND GIVES FRANNY A HUG. PING PONG GOES INTO A RAGE.

FRANNY　　　See he still loves me! Shoosh up Ping! Dad are you coming to Dolly and Teddy's wedding?

RICHARD　　　Again?

FRANNY　　　Dolly has a new haircut.

RICHARD　　　Sorry Possum, I'm waiting for a call.

FRANNY SITS AND PLAYS WITH HER TOYS. SHE GIVES TEDDY A HUG. PARROT MAN TRIES TO GET HER ATTENTION.

THE PHONE RINGS.

RICHARD　　　Nice try, mate.

THE PHONE KEEPS RINGING. RICHARD STARES PARROT MAN DOWN.

IT GOES TO ANSWERING MACHINE. BEEP.

VOICE　　　Hi there, was just hoping to get onto Richard McGrath...

RICHARD SCRAMBLES TOWARDS THE PHONE.

RICHARD　　　Hello this is Richard speaking. Yes. Yes exactly right. I completely agree with you...

FRANNY, DESPERATE FOR RICHARD'S ATTENTION, GIVES HIM A KISS ON THE CHEEK. RICHARD TRIES TO SUBDUE HER WITH A PAT ON THE HEAD. PARROT MAN SQUAWKS JEALOUSLY.

RICHARD　　　Sorry what? The noise? It's my daughter's pet cockatiel. It's distracting isn't it?

RICHARD　　　(*WHISPERING*) Franny, can you please calm him down?

FRANNY SULKS OVER TO HIS CAGE AND TRIES TO CALM HIM. PARROT MAN SQUAWKS LOUDER.

RICHARD　　　Yep, yep, sorry. I'll shut him up. Just give me a second.

RICHARD COVERS THE PHONE.

RICHARD　　　Why won't he shut up?

ACT 2   Scene 2

FRANNY   I don't know! He's got food and water. I'm trying to play with my toys, it's not fair.

PING SQUAWKS LOUDER STILL. RICHARD TAKES A DEEP BREATH.

RICHARD   Franny. Dad's on an extremely important call. I really need you to calm him down. Remember how much he loves doing that dance on your hand?

FRANNY   Mum says that's not allowed anymore.

RICHARD   Mum would want this phone call to go well. Come on, Sweetie, it'll only take a second.

FRANNY FIDGETS, UNCOMFORTABLE.

RICHARD   I'll tell you what, as soon as I'm finished on the phone, we'll go to the toy store. Pick Dolly out a new dress.

PAUSE.

RICHARD   We'll get a Happy Meal on the way home.

FRANNY RELUCTANTLY APPROACHES THE CAGE. RICHARD GOES BACK TO THE PHONE.

RICHARD   Sorry about that. Where were we?

Scene 2

RICHARD IS STILL ON THE PHONE.

RICHARD   Thank you so much. You won't regret it.

RICHARD HANGS UP. HE SMILES. HIS SMILE DRAINS. HE WALKS OVER TO THE CAGE AND PULLS OFF THE SHEET. PING PONG AND UGBOOT ARE ASLEEP. FRANNY SITS IN THE CORNER OF THE CAGE.

RICHARD   Are you ready to go, Darling?

FRANNY   I need the Dettol.

THE PARROT MAN OPENS HIS EYES.

PING PONG   Formative years.

RICHARD   In the bathroom, Sweetheart. I'll wait here.

FRANNY EXITS.

RICHARD   You're an animal! An innocent animal.

PING PONG   You're an animal. Formative years. Formative years.

Scene 3

RICHARD SITS CROSS-LEGGED. FRANNY CONDUCTS HER ELABORATE TOY WEDDING.

JOAN ENTERS. SMILES. TAKES A SEAT NEXT TO RICHARD.

JOAN	Do you remember doing anything like this as a kid?
RICHARD	Playing with toys?
JOAN	Fantasising about marriage?
RICHARD	Can you imagine my father if he found me doing something like this?
JOAN	But when you were alone?
RICHARD	I always knew I'd get married, but it was just a fact of life. Nothing to get excited about.
JOAN	Were you excited on our wedding day?
RICHARD	Of course. But that wasn't make-believe. Did you?
JOAN	Get excited on our wedding day?
RICHARD	Yeah.
JOAN	I did… But it made me feel sick.
RICHARD	You never told me you were sick that day?
JOAN	I wasn't sick. I felt sick. I played this game a lot as a kid. I had so much invested in it.
RICHARD	You were disappointed?
JOAN	You were pleasantly surprised?

THERE'S A SUDDEN RUFFLING OF FEATHERS. SQUAWKING. PING PONG AND UGBOOT DANCE.

RICHARD	What a day for romance, eh, Franny?

FRANNY DROPS TEDDY AND DOLLY.

FRANNY	Ping Pong?

PING PONG SQUAWKS LOUDLY THEN GOES BACK TO UGBOOT.

FRANNY	What are they doing?
JOAN	Dancing, Sweetie.
FRANNY	But he danced with me today.

RICHARD TURNS AWAY FROM FRANNY AND JOAN. HE PRETENDS TO BE DOING SOMETHING.

ACT 2 Scene 3

FRANNY　　Will Ugboot need the Dettol? Because it's all gone.

JOAN　　I told you that Ping Pong wasn't allowed to do that anymore. Why did you disobey your father and me? Richard did you know?

FRANNY　　Dad said I was helping.

JOAN　　There's some Starbursts in my handbag, go find them.

FRANNY NODS. SHE EXITS.

JOAN GLARES AT RICHARD. RAGE BREATHING.

RICHARD　　Starbursts Joan? I thought we decided…

JOAN STARES HIM DOWN.

RICHARD　　I got a VERY important phone call. He wouldn't shut up. He was imitating the phone ring, and he KNEW it was an important phone call!

RICHARD POINTS FURIOUSLY AT PARROT MAN. JOAN POINTS FURIOUSLY AT RICHARD.

JOAN　　He's an evil genius now? But when he was getting off on our daughter "birds will be birds"?

RICHARD　　This seemed so calculated. And then he spoke…

JOAN　　He spoke? What'd he say? "Polly want a cracker"?

RICHARD　　No. "Formative years".

JOAN LAUGHS. GROWS ICY. SILENCE.

JOAN　　Even the paedophile parrot thinks we're bad parents.

FRANNY RE-ENTERS, UNSEEN.

RICHARD　　It won't happen again. He's moved on to Ugboot. Tossed Franny aside like yesterday's bread.

JOAN WALKS UP TO UGBOOT.

JOAN　　I'm so sorry girl.

RICHARD　　Better than our girl.

JOAN　　Shut the fuck up.

FRANNY　　Shut the fuck up!

JOAN AND RICHARD TURN TO FRANNY.

RICHARD　　What did you say?

FRANNY　　Shut the fuck up!

RICHARD　　Apologise to your mother right now.

JOAN　　Just leave it.

Love Bird

ACT 2   Scene 4

Joan storms out. Richard sits down, exhausted.

Franny trembles. She goes into her fort and buries her face in the pillows.

RICHARD   You can't talk to your mother like that.

FRANNY   She said it to you. I hate her.

RICHARD   Well she loves you. Unconditionally. We both do. Nobody will ever love you as much as your mum and I do.

FRANNY   Nobody?

Richard and Franny look at Ping.

RICHARD   Not the same way.

FRANNY   Do you love Mum unconditionally? Even when she tells you to shut the fuck up?

RICHARD   Franny. It's a different kind of… of course.

Scene 4

Loud squawking can be heard.

Ping Pong and Ugboot stand centre stage. They are both men in parrot suits now.

Franny wakes up.

FRANNY   Ugboot? You're beautiful. Mum!

Joan enters.

JOAN   It's really early Fran.

FRANNY   Ugboot isn't ugly anymore.

Joan turns to the cage.

JOAN   Please no. Richard!

Richard enters, brushing his teeth.

RICHARD   Whauuu?

She points to the cage. Richard spits toothpaste.

FRANNY   I thought Bill said girl birds were ugly?

JOAN   I think Bill doesn't know as much about birds as he made out.

FRANNY   I don't understand.

JOAN   Ugboot is a boy.

FRANNY	But they're doing the silly dance.
JOAN	Yes.
FRANNY	Boys can't make eggs with other boys?
JOAN	No.
FRANNY	Then Prince Ping Pong's instincts aren't very good.
JOAN	Almost as bad as Bill's.

JOAN SITS FRANNY DOWN.

JOAN	Franny, not all sex is about making babies.
FRANNY	Huh…
RICHARD	They weren't doing s… s… silly dancing!

RICHARD PICKS UP A BIG BUNCH OF FEATHERS. ALMOST RELIEVED.

RICHARD	They've been at each other.
JOAN	There you go Franny, they were never dancing, they were fighting.

FRANNY LOOKS AT THE FEATHERS.

FRANNY	Why do they look so similar?
RICHARD	Ping Pong and Ugboot?
FRANNY	Doing sex and fighting.

SILENCE.

RICHARD	They're animals, Possum.

JOAN PUSHES THE CAGE TOWARD THE WINDOW.

JOAN	I'm not running a cage fighting ring in my living room. Say goodbye Franny.
FRANNY	You can't! They're mine.
JOAN	If you don't let them go they'll keep hurting each other.
FRANNY	If they fly away they won't be my friends anymore.
JOAN	These stupid birds are not your friends. The cage is driving them insane. It's not right. None of this is right.

JOAN YANKS THE WINDOW OPEN AND OPENS THE CAGE DOOR. UGBOOT FLIES AWAY. PING PONG WATCHES AFTER HIM BUT DOESN'T MOVE.

JOAN SHAKES THE CAGE.

JOAN	Go on. Shoo.
RICHARD	He's got Stockholm syndrome.

RICHARD PICKS UP THE COCKATIEL MANUAL.

ACT 2 Scene 4

RICHARD Apparently cockatiels mate for life. (*BEAT*) You were right Possum, he still loves you.

FRANNY Unconditionally?

PING PONG NODS. HE AND FRANNY RUN TO EACH OTHER. THEY EMBRACE.

FRANNY We're going to live happily ever after.

ACT 3

Scene 1

PING PONG PACES AROUND HIS CAGE. HE PREENS HIS FEATHERS. HE LOOKS IN THE MIRROR. HE PREENS AGAIN. HE PACES. HE PICKS UP A GIANT SUNFLOWER SEED. HE PEELS IT. HE BITES IT. THROWS IT ON THE FLOOR. PACES. HE RINGS HIS BELL. THE DOOR HANDLE TURNS. HE STOPS, STANDS UP STRAIGHT.

FRANNY ENTERS. OLDER. 14-ISH. SHE'S TEXTING.

PING PONG CHIRPS.

JOAN	Franny, can you check if Ping has fresh water?
FRANNY	He doesn't!
JOAN	Can you change it?
FRANNY	I have so much homework!
JOAN	I'll call the RSPCA and report you.
FRANNY	I'll call child services and report you.

FRANNY EXITS.

JOAN ENTERS, SLIGHTLY WORN. SHE PULLS OUT HIS WATER DISH, IT'S DISGUSTING.

JOAN   Did nobody ever teach you not to shit where you eat?

PING PONG STARES BLANKLY. JOAN TRIES TO WHISTLE TO HIM. HE LOOKS PAST HER TO THE DOOR.

JOAN   You're wasting your time with that one.

RICHARD ENTERS, TEXTING. DOESN'T LOOK UP.

RICHARD	How long 'til dinner?
JOAN	I'm going out actually. There's this exhibition, did you want to…
RICHARD	I'll order in.
JOAN	Something with vegetables, Franny's still growing.

RICHARD EXITS. JOAN LOOKS IN PING PONG'S MIRROR, PUTS ON LIPSTICK AND EXITS.

THE ROOM IS EMPTY. PING PONG IMITATES DIALLING. HE RINGS. HE RINGS OUT.

Love Bird

ACT 3   Scene 1

PING PONG   Beeeeeeeeeeeepppppppp.
SILENCE. NOBODY LEAVES A MESSAGE. HE STARTS AGAIN.
FRANNY AND RICHARD ENTER, BOTH TEXTING.

RICHARD   Your little trick doesn't work anymore, does it, mate?

PING PONG STARTS RINGING AGAIN.

FRANNY   Ping, nobody has a landline anymore.
RICHARD   Once they've learnt something, that's it, it's in there forever.
PING PONG   Formative years.
FRANNY   He's so random.

BEAT.

RICHARD   I've gotta go out for a while. Will you be okay to hold the fort?

THEY LOOK AT WHAT'S LEFT OF HER DILAPIDATED FORT.

FRANNY   Owls?
RICHARD   Tawny frogmouths. Night's the best time for them.
FRANNY   What happened to the powerful owls?
RICHARD   I already checked them off.
FRANNY   But are they still living on the ridge?
RICHARD   I assume so.
FRANNY   Still mating for life?
RICHARD   If they're still alive. Since when are you so interested in owls?
FRANNY   I'm not. Have fun Dad.

RICHARD EXITS. SO DOES FRANNY.

FRANNY'S PHONE RINGS—SOME STUPID CUSTOMISED RING TONE. SHE RUNS BACK INTO THE ROOM. PING PONG'S CREST RISES. HE TWEETS SWEETLY AT HER. SHE IGNORES HIM AND ANSWERS THE PHONE. HE ATTEMPTS TO IMITATE THE NEW RING TONE.

FRANNY   Hello? Oh hi. Sweet. Yeah I'm home. No I'm on my own.

FRANNY GIGGLES. SHE LOOKS INTO PING PONG'S MIRROR AND APPLIES SOME LIP GLOSS. PING KEEPS STEPPING BETWEEN HER AND THE MIRROR.

KNOCK KNOCK.

FRANNY ANSWERS THE DOOR. IT'S A TEENAGE BOY.

FRANNY   Hi.

ACT 3 Scene 1

BOY Hi.

PING PONG IS ON EDGE.

BOY Well can I come in?

FRANNY Sure. I've never had a boy inside before... Ugh I shouldn't have told you that.

BOY Maybe tonight's a good time for first times?

FRANNY Do you want something to drink?

BOY What've you got?

FRANNY Tea. Cordial. Water. Strawberry Quik.

BOY Lame.

THE BOY PICKS UP A CASK OF WINE.

FRANNY Mum just uses that in risotto I think. It's been there for at least a million years.

BOY It's still better than cordial.

FRANNY Okay. But it's raspberry.

THE BOY LEADS FRANNY ONTO THE COUCH. HE TRICKLES THE CASK WINE INTO HIS OWN MOUTH. THEN INTO HERS. MOST OF IT MISSES.

BOY What do you say?

HE LEANS CLOSE, TEASING HER.

FRANNY Thank you.

BOY Good girl.

THEY KISS.

PING PONG FLAPS AND SQUAWKS.

BOY Your bird's a bit of a perv.

FRANNY He just gets a bit jealous sometimes.

BOY Why, is he your husband or something?

FRANNY No!

THE BOY SLIDES HIS HAND FURTHER SOUTH.

FRANNY What are you doing?

BOY Whatever you want me to do?

FRANNY GOES TO TALK. HE KISSES HER INSTEAD. PING PONG SQUAWKS FURIOUSLY.

BOY Is there any way you can shut that bird up? It's a bit of a turn off tbh.

ACT 3　　　　　　　　　　　　　　　　　　　　　　　Scene 2

FRANNY　　　　I'm sorry.

PING BEATS THE CAGE, SQUAWKS AND FLAPS.

BOY　　　　　 Put that sheet over him.

FRANNY　　　　Won't help.

BOY　　　　　 My brother's picking me up from the corner store in half an hour and this is lame as fuck. Maybe I should just leave?

FRANNY　　　　Please don't. Why don't you just go outside for one second.

BOY　　　　　 Fine.

THE BOY EXITS.

FRANNY APPROACHES PING PONG.

FRANNY　　　　Shhhh.

Scene 2

FRANNY WASHES HER HANDS WITH DETTOL.
THE SHEET IS OVER PING'S CAGE. HIS SILHOUETTE SMOKES A CIGARETTE.
THE BOY ENTERS.

BOY　　　　　 My brother's almost here.

FRANNY　　　　I'm sorry.

BOY　　　　　 I guess I'm looking for someone a little more mature.

FRANNY　　　　I am mature. It's just that fucking bird.

BOY　　　　　 You sure? I was worried there was something wrong with you.

FRANNY　　　　Like what?

BOY　　　　　 Well is there?

FRANNY　　　　No.

BOY　　　　　 I guess I can stay a bit longer.

THE BOY TAKES THE SHEET OFF PING PONG'S CAGE. HE THROWS IT OVER THEIR LAPS.

FRANNY　　　　He'll be watching now.

BOY　　　　　 So?

HE PULLS HER HAND UNDER THE SHEETS.

ACT 3   Scene 2

BOY   Yeah that's it baby. Yeah.

PING PONG BASHES HIS BEAK AGAINST THE CAGE.

BOY   Ow. Owww. Ahh ahhh what the fuck are you doing! It burns. Why does it burn?

FRANNY   Shit. It must be the Dettol. It's peppermint.

BOY   What the fuck?

FRANNY   I just washed my hands.

BOY   What the fuck! Dettol? I bet you've given me herpes or some shit.

FRANNY   It's just hand sanitiser.

BOY   How stupid do you think I am? Where's my phone, I need to tell everyone about this.

FRANNY   But I didn't…

BOY   Slut.

THE BOY EXITS.

FRANNY SITS THERE FOR A MOMENT. STUNNED. PING PONG STARTS RINGING AGAIN.

FRANNY WALKS TOWARDS HIM.

PING PONG   beeeeeeeeep.

FRANNY   This is all your fault.

FRANNY SQUEEZES THE DETTOL ONTO HIS HEAD. HE SQUAWKS IN DISTRESS.

FRANNY   Stupid fucking bird!

JOAN ENTERS, DISHEVELLED.

JOAN   What have you done to that poor bird?

FRANNY BREAKS.

FRANNY   I hate him.

JOAN   Franny, what's happened?

FRANNY   Humans can't get STIs from birds can they?

JOAN   You mean from when you were little?

PAUSE.

FRANNY   It's what the Dettol was for, right? Birds are full of diseases.

JOAN   Well yes. But I don't think… What's wrong? Are you itchy down there? You've been changing your undies every day?

Love Bird

ACT 3   Scene 2

FRANNY   Mum!

JOAN   Well, there's something you're not telling me.

FRANNY   It's too embarrassing.

JOAN   Is it a boy?

FRANNY   Maybe.

JOAN   Fucking boys.

FRANNY   Mum!

JOAN   Sorry, you might as well just tell me.

FRANNY   I had a boy over. Just for 20 minutes.

JOAN   Too much can happen in 20 minutes.

FRANNY   It can if you don't have a horny, jealous bird on your back the whole time.

JOAN   What happened?

FRANNY   He threatened to leave if Ping didn't shut up. So I told him to wait outside.

JOAN   Oh God.

FRANNY   I washed my hands with Dettol just like you said. And then the boy wanted to… You know? But I made his thing hurt.

JOAN   He made you touch his penis?!

FRANNY   I wanted to. I think. I'm not sure. I mean he didn't tell me I had to. But… And now he says he's gonna tell everyone I gave him herpes.

FRANNY SOBS.

JOAN   No he won't.

FRANNY   But what if I did give him herpes?

JOAN   Ping Pong doesn't have herpes.

FRANNY   That's what I said. He wouldn't believe me.

JOAN   Little cunt.

FRANNY   Mum!

JOAN   He's not going to tell people you gave him herpes because he's not going to tell everyone he has herpes.

FRANNY   But he doesn't! I don't. I can't believe I was going to… I'm so ashamed.

JOAN   Ashamed?

FRANNY	That I was going to give him that…
JOAN	It's not something you give away. It will always belong to you, no matter how often you try and offload it.
FRANNY	I don't understand.
JOAN	I think when I was your age, I thought I had to try and give myself to someone who would value me. That I would unburden myself. But Franny, it doesn't matter how much someone else loves you, you will always be your own burden.
FRANNY	He doesn't own part of me forever?
JOAN	Not even if he thinks he does. You're stuck with you. All the pieces, jumbled, and only you can figure out how they'll fit together.
FRANNY	Don't tell Dad.

FRANNY EXITS.
PING PONG RINGS.

JOAN	Weren't you listening? You're on your own. We all are.

JOAN EXITS.
PING PONG LOOKS IN HIS MIRROR. HE KEEPS RINGING.

Scene 3

RICHARD LIES IN BED. JOAN GETS CHANGED BEHIND A SCREEN.

RICHARD	She didn't let him in our room did she? She didn't let him do anything to her?
JOAN	To her? Like what, Richard?
RICHARD	Don't make me.
JOAN	You assume every boy's aim is to defile your daughter?
RICHARD	Every 14-year-old boy, it's how they're wired.
JOAN	The odds aren't in her favour.
RICHARD	No they're not! Did you ground her?
JOAN	What?
RICHARD	Did you do anything?
JOAN	Nup.
RICHARD	How will she learn?

ACT 3   Scene 3

JOAN   Learn what?
RICHARD   Not to let boys have their way.
JOAN   That's fucked.
RICHARD   What boys want is disgusting.

RICHARD GRABS JOAN AROUND THE WAIST.

JOAN   What about what girls want?
RICHARD   To madly, on a pile of rose petals, make love to Michael Bublé?
JOAN   To be fucked hard in the arse and have my hair pulled at the roots? (*BEAT*) Don't split infinitives.
RICHARD   Is that what you want?
JOAN   It might just be what men want us to want. Too late for me to know the difference. But it's not too late…

RICHARD KISSES HER.

JOAN   Am I supposed to forego what I want just because men are disgusting?

RICHARD PULLS JOAN'S HAIR.

RICHARD   Does that get you wet?
JOAN   Does it make you hard?
RICHARD   Yeah.
JOAN   Really?
RICHARD   I think so. I mean, I am hard. Does it make you…
JOAN   I'm wet.

RICHARD KISSES HER AGAIN.

JOAN   What if deep down what you really want is for me to paint your face in my menstrual blood and stick my tongue in your belly button. While Bublé watches. You've just been programmed to want to pull my hair and cum on my face?
RICHARD   Joan, we've got a hard cock and a wet pussy between us, isn't that enough?
JOAN   Almost.

JOAN GRABS THE VIBRATING EGG, SWITCHES IT ON AND HANDS IT TO RICHARD. OR MAYBE RICHARD TURNS IT ON HIMSELF. HE LOWERS IT TOWARDS JOAN.

Love Bird

Scene 4

RICHARD ENTERS THE LIVING ROOM WITH HIS BIRD ENCYCLOPAEDIA.

RICHARD   Well done on the minty burning sensation. Kid had it coming.

RICHARD OPENS THE CAGE DOOR. PING PONG AND RICHARD TAKE A SEAT ON THE COUCH. RICHARD PULLS OUT HIS BAG OF DORITOS, OFFERS SOME TO PING. HE OPENS HIS BIRD BOOK.

RICHARD   See this guy, the superb fairy wren? The first bird Bill and I ever checked off. I'd seen birds before obviously, but he showed me how to really see them: plumage, wing-span, beak-shape. I've crossed off most of the birds in this book, but I only really remember the ones I saw with Bill. Still, things change, people change. Grow apart. You know?

PING WHISTLES AND LOOKS IN THE OTHER DIRECTION. RICHARD SIGHS.

RICHARD   I wanted to check if she was okay, still the same. It seems silly now.

RICHARD GETS UP TO EXIT. HE SWITCHES ON THE RADIO.

RICHARD   To keep you company.

RICHARD EXITS.

PING BEGINS HIS RINGING CYCLE.

A TELEPHONE-THEMED POP SONG PLAYS ON THE RADIO. THE SONG, AND PING, HARMONISE.

FRANNY CREEPS IN THE FRONT DOOR, DISHEVELLED. SHE FLOPS DOWN ON THE COUCH AND LOOKS OUT INTO SPACE. THE POP SONG PLAYS AND PING CONTINUES TO RING. FRANNY LOOKS AT HER PHONE. NOTHING.

FRANNY   Bastard.

SHE THROWS THE PHONE ACROSS THE ROOM AND CURLS UP ON THE COUCH. THE MUSIC FADES OUT.

PING'S RINGING CONTINUES.

Scene 5

PING PONG IS STILL RINGING, BETWEEN COUGHING AND SPLUTTERING.
FRANNY WAKES UP.

FRANNY   What's wrong with you?

JOAN ENTERS.

FRANNY   Mum, something's wrong with Ping.

JOAN LOOKS IN HIS CAGE.

JOAN   When was the last time you changed his water?

FRANNY   I thought you usually did that.

JOAN   For fuck sake Franny.

FRANNY TEARS UP.

JOAN   Ping is sick, he could die, because you couldn't be bothered getting him fresh water. Sometimes you have to take responsibility for your actions Francine!

FRANNY   I had sex.

JOAN   What?

FRANNY   I'm sorry, Mum.

JOAN   Franny... Shit. Did you use protection?

FRANNY   We're out of Dettol.

JOAN   What?!

FRANNY   Kidding. But it hurts a little.

JOAN   It wasn't with that same boy? That little piece of shit.

RICHARD ENTERS.

RICHARD   What are you girls conspiring about?

JOAN   You and I are going to the chemist, apparently we're out of Dettol.

RICHARD   Do we need it this second?

JOAN   Yep. Dettol. And other things... Franny, you stay with Ping.

RICHARD   He looks terrible... Should I call Bill?

JOAN & FRANNY   No.

JOAN AND RICHARD EXIT. FRANNY APPROACHES THE CAGE.

ACT 3   Scene 6

FRANNY   Are you dying? Can I make you stop dying?

PING PONG TWEETS IN EXHAUSTION.

FRANNY   I'm so sorry.

PARROT MAN COUGHS AND PICKS UP A CIGARETTE. FRANNY LEANS PAST THE PUPPET AND LIGHTS THE MAN'S CIGARETTE.

FRANNY   Why don't I read to you. Mum threw out the readers, but I have these.

FRANNY OPENS A MAGAZINE.

FRANNY   Dear Dolly Doctor…

Scene 6

PING PONG (PUPPET) LIES DEAD ON THE FLOOR OF THE BIRD CAGE. THE MAN IS GONE.

FRANNY PULLS THE FINAL SHEET FROM THE PILLOW FORT AND LAYS IT OVER HIS BODY.

SHE WASHES HER HANDS WITH DETTOL. SHE DIALS A NUMBER.

FRANNY   Dad, can you get me Maccas on the way home. Not a Happy Meal, a Quarter Pounder Meal with a chocolate thick shake as the drink. And some nuggets. Can you please just do it, Dad?

About the Author

Georgie Harriss is a creative writer passionate about telling stories that are intimate, interrogative and strange. She was born in Albury and is now based in Melbourne. She holds an Honours degree in Screenwriting from the Victorian College of the Arts.

In 2016, Georgie was selected as one of Lonely Company's writers-in-residence. Her play, *Love Bird*, which she developed during this residency, enjoyed successful runs at both The Butterfly Club and La Mama in 2018.

Georgie has been the recipient of an ATYP Fresh Ink National Mentorship, a Tessa Waters Mentorship and a Wheeler Centre Hot Desk Fellowship. Her writing has been presented by Red Stitch and Theatre Works. With Amelia Newman, she is currently co-artistic director of Curtain Kill, a text-centred theatre company dedicated to telling queer and feminist stories with the complexity and joy they deserve.

Georgie is currently a PhD candidate in Creative Writing at Monash University. Her research explores queer narratological approaches to writing lived experiences of trauma.

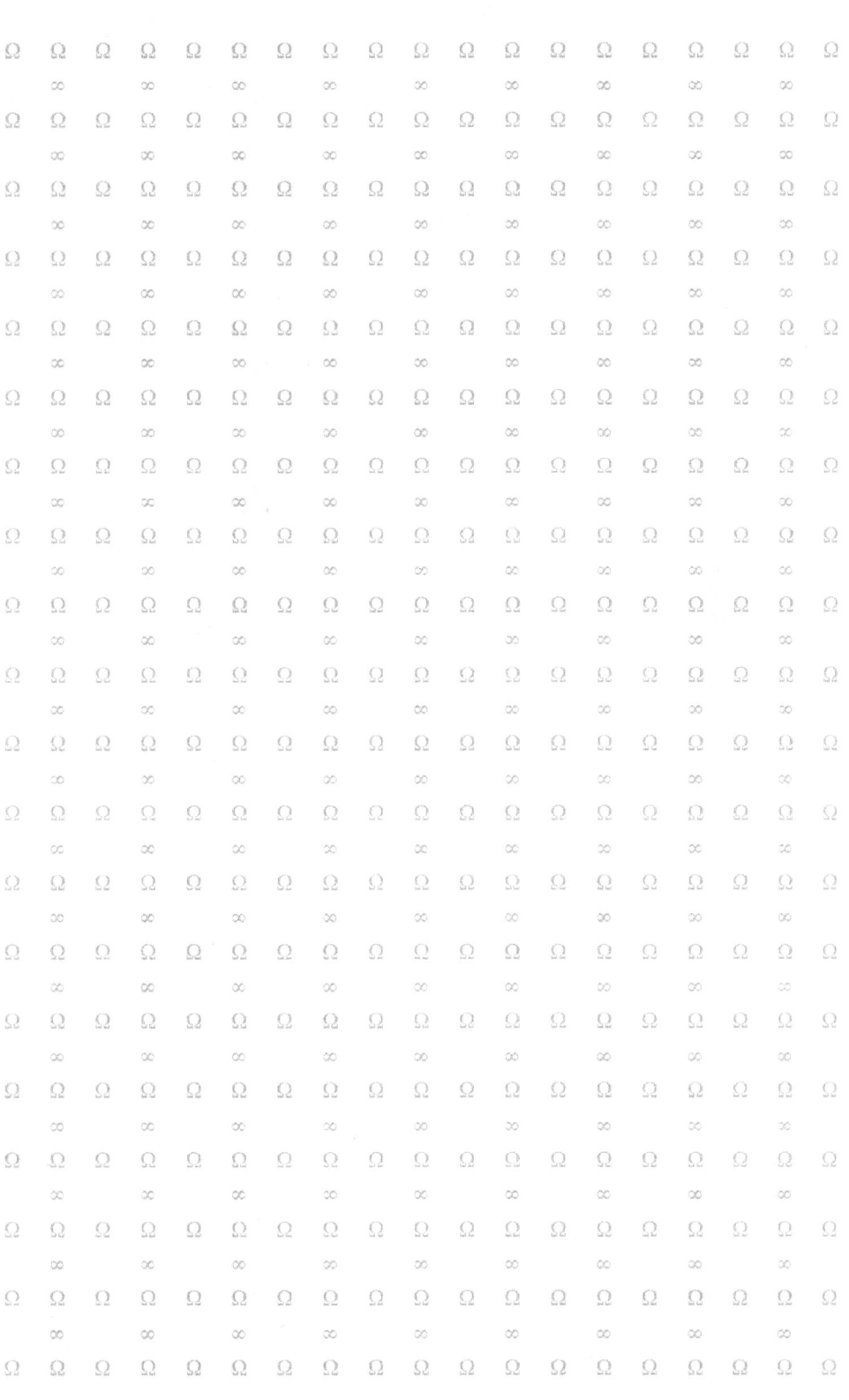

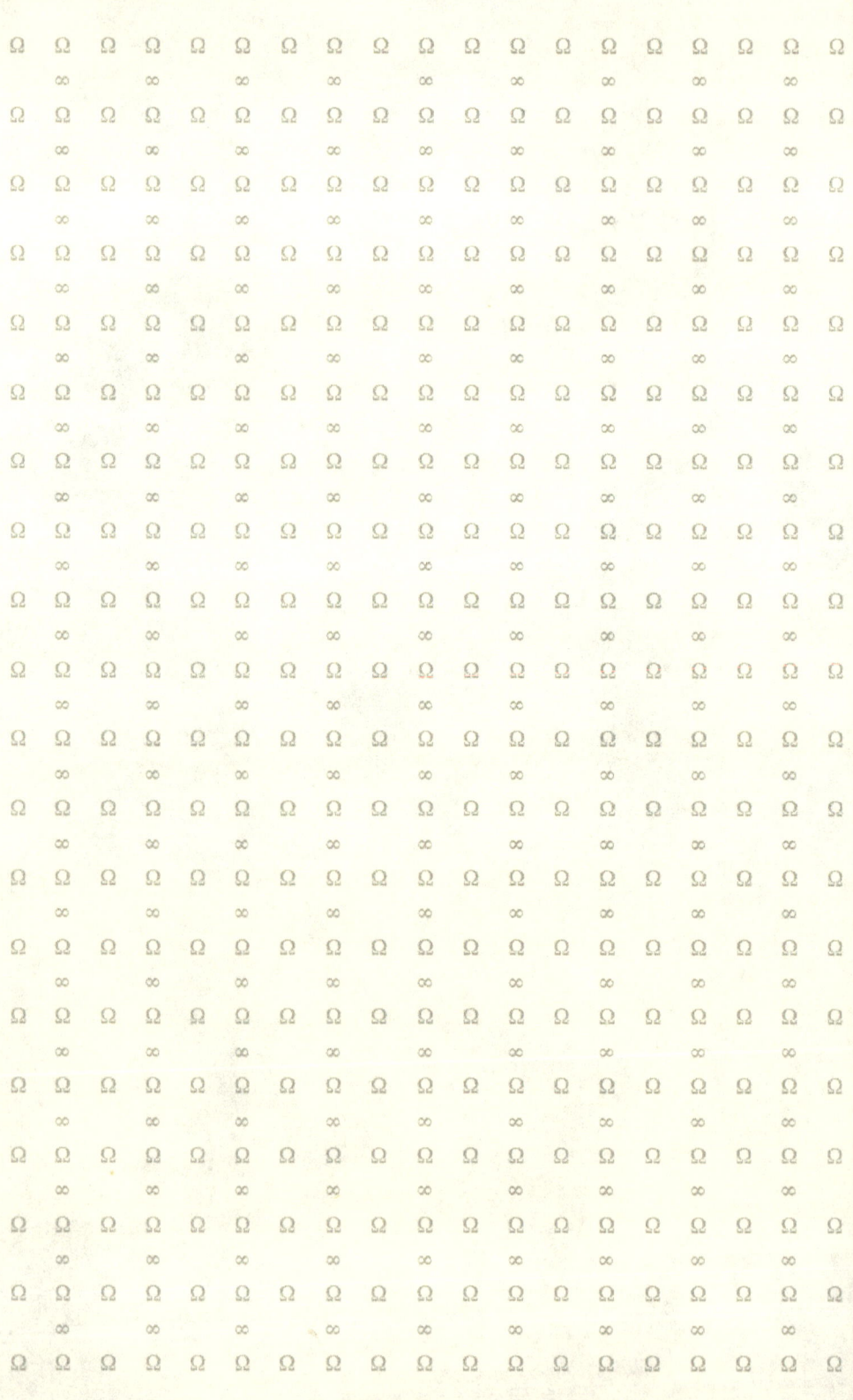

www.ingramcontent.com/pod-product-compliance
Lightning Source LLC
Chambersburg PA
CBHW022022290426
44109CB00015B/1269